TICKET TO THE
WORLD SERIES

MARTIN GITLIN

ADMIT ONE

THE BIG GAME
YOUR FRONT ROW SEAT

45TH PARALLEL PRESS

Published in the United States of America by Cherry Lake Publishing Group
Ann Arbor, Michigan
www.cherrylakepublishing.com

Reading Adviser: Beth Walker Gambro, MS Ed., Reading Consultant, Yorkville, IL
Book Designer: Jen Wahi

Photo Credits: Cover: Cover: © Jerry Coli/Dreamstime.com; page 5: © Jerry Coli/Dreamstime.com; page 7: © Conor P. Fitzgerald/Shutterstock; page 9: © Jerry Coli/Dreamstime.com; page 13: © Library of Congress/LC-USZ62-98072; page 15: © Richard Paul Kane/Shutterstock; page 17: © Jerry Coli/Dreamstime.com; page 18: © Matt Trommer/Shutterstock; page 20 (top): © Conor P. Fitzgerald/Shutterstock; page 20 (bottom): © Jerry Coli/Dreamstime.com; page 22 (top): © Keeton Gale/Shutterstock; page 22 (bottom): © Hendrickson Photography/Shutterstock; page 25: © Library of Congress/LC-USZC4-6147; page 26 (top): © Jerry Coli/Dreamstime.com; page 26 (bottom): © Debby Wong/Shutterstock

45th Parallel Press is an imprint of Cherry Lake Publishing Group.

Library of Congress Cataloging-in-Publication Data

Names: Gitlin, Martin, author.
Title: Ticket to the World Series / By Martin Gitlin.
Description: Ann Arbor, Michigan : Cherry Lake Publishing, [2023] | Series: The big game | Audience: Grades 4-6 | Summary: "Who has won the World Series? How did they make it to the final game? Written as high interest with struggling readers in mind, this series includes considerate vocabulary, engaging content and fascinating facts, clear text and formatting, and compelling photos. Educational sidebars include extra fun facts and information about each game. Includes table of contents, glossary, index, and author biography"-- Provided by publisher.
Identifiers: LCCN 2022039915 | ISBN 9781668919538 (hardcover) | ISBN 9781668920558 (paperback) | ISBN 9781668921883 (ebook) | ISBN 9781668923214 (pdf)
Subjects: LCSH: World Series (Baseball)--History--Juvenile literature. | Baseball--United States--History--Juvenile literature. | Baseball--United States--Miscellanea--Juvenile literature. | Baseball--Tournaments--United States--History--Juvenile literature.
Classification: LCC GV878.4 .G57 2023 | DDC 796.357/64609--dc23/eng/20220901
LC record available at https://lccn.loc.gov/2022039915

Cherry Lake Publishing would like to acknowledge the work of the Partnership for 21st Century Learning, a network of Battelle for Kids. Please visit http://www.battelleforkids.org/networks/p21

Printed in the United States of America
Corporate Graphics

Table of Contents

Introduction

The World Series is the biggest battle in Major League Baseball (MLB). It starts every year in late October. The winner is the MLB champion. The event is also called the Fall Classic.

Many MLB clubs compete in the playoffs. Those games are played after the regular season. They are played between teams that won the most games. But only 2 teams reach the World Series. One is from the American League. The other is from the National League. They are pennant winners.

The 2 teams host every World Series game in their ballparks. The first to win 4 games is the World Series champion.

Ozzie Smith (known as the Wizard of Oz) of the St. Louis Cardinals is up to bat. The Cardinals have won the World Series 11 times.

The Fall Classic features the best teams ever. It also spotlights the sport's best players. Many people believe it is the greatest sporting event in the United States.

Shohei Ohtani of the Los Angeles Angels is a modern player who has been compared to Babe Ruth!

An Amazing History

The seeds of the World Series were planted in 1901. That year, the American League (AL) was founded. It competed with the National League. The National League (NL) had been around since 1876.

Both leagues tried to attract the best players. Fans wanted to see the top talent. Winning games drew people to the ballparks.

Ticket sales were the main source of income for team owners. There were no radio or TV stations. There was no money from broadcast rights. That is money paid by TV stations to show a game.

Owners wanted new ways to make money. They created one in 1903. It was the World Series.

The New York Yankees leap for joy as they celebrate winning the World Series in 2000!

The owners believed a battle between champions would attract fans. They thought it would grow interest in the game. They were right. The World Series became the biggest event in U.S. sports.

Several teams ruled baseball in the early 1900s. The same clubs often won pennants year after year.

The first was the Chicago Cubs. That team beat the Detroit Tigers in the 1907 and 1908 World Series.

The American League then took over. Its Philadelphia club won 3 titles in 4 years. The Athletics won an amazing 12 of 16 World Series games during that time.

Soon AL champion Boston gained control. The Red Sox won 3 titles from 1915 to 1918. An incredible pitcher helped the Red Sox win. His name was Babe Ruth. But in 1919, Ruth moved to the New York Yankees.

Ruth did not only help that team win titles. He changed the game and the World Series. But he did not do it as a pitcher. He changed baseball with his booming bat.

☆ The modern World Series was born in 1903. But that wasn't the first baseball championship. Several other versions were played in the late 1800s.

☆ All of them involved the American Association. That league competed against the National League. Their champions played in early versions of the World Series. The first was in 1884. The NL Providence Grays defeated the New York Metropolitans.

☆ The American Association went out of business in 1891. The American League was born 10 years later.

WAY BACK WHEN

The Yankees Dynasty

Baseball was in its dead ball era when Ruth arrived. That means baseballs did not travel as far. Soon Ruth began doing what others did not. He hit a lot of home runs. That forced the Red Sox to change his role. Ruth became a full-time hitter.

Ruth turned the Yankees into a power. The team added other home-run hitters. Another well-known hitter was Lou Gehrig. Ruth and Gehrig helped New York start a dynasty. That is a team that wins many titles.

The Yankees won the World Series 4 times from 1923 to 1932. Most believe they peaked in 1927. They won an amazing 110 games that year. They won 4 in a row against Pittsburgh in the World Series.

Babe Ruth is known as one of the greatest baseball players of all time. He hit 714 home runs during his career.

The Yankees became even better after Ruth retired in 1935. Hitter Joe DiMaggio replaced him. His teams won every title from 1936 to 1939. Even World War II did not stop the Yankees. They earned titles in 1941 and 1943.

It was hard to imagine the Yankees could become more powerful. Yet they did. They won 6 pennants from 1947 to 1953. They won each of those Fall Classics.

By that time a new Yankees star had replaced DiMaggio. His name was Mickey Mantle. Mantle helped his team win one pennant after another. New York played in every World Series but 2 from 1949 to 1964. And they won 9 of them.

Other teams became baseball powers after that. But none would match the run of the Yankees. Never again would any team win more than 3 straight World Series.

David Robertson is a pitcher who has played for many teams in the MLB. Here he is with the New York Yankees.

Expansion and Playoffs

Reaching the World Series became harder in 1962. The American and National Leagues added 2 teams. Both leagues now had 10 clubs.

The Yankees' dominance ended in 1965. New teams emerged as powers. But rarely did any team win back-to-back titles.

One reason was expanded playoffs. The leagues divided into 2 divisions in 1969. A playoff series followed the regular season. Only the winner advanced to the World Series. The result was a new champion almost every year.

There were exceptions. The Oakland Athletics won every World Series from 1972 to 1974. The Yankees bounced back to take titles in 1977 and 1978. The Toronto Blue Jays won titles in 1992 and 1993. Then the Yankees won every title from 1998 to 2000.

Jose Canseco swings the bat for the Oakland Athletics. He played for them from 1985—1992. The Athletics won 3 World Series in a row a decade earlier.

The St. Louis Cardinals won multiple World Series. Here they are in 2011 in a pre-season game against the Florida Marlins. They won the World Series later that year!

The game had changed greatly by then. Several new teams were added to both leagues. More playoffs made it harder to reach the World Series.

After 2000, some World Series teams snagged repeat titles. St. Louis had won more titles than any National League club. And the Cardinals continued to win. They won in both 2006 and 2011. The Yankees earned one in 2009.

The World Series has been canceled only once since 1905. It was not played in 1994.

 That was a terrible year for baseball. The players and owners could not agree on many issues. So the players went on strike. They refused to play.

 An agreement could not be reached. So MLB canceled the 1994 World Series. It remains perhaps the most shameful period for baseball.

A BIT OF TRIVIA

Camilo Doval of the San Francisco Giants sends a fast pitch during a game against the Colorado Rockies. He can pitch up to 104.5 miles per hour.

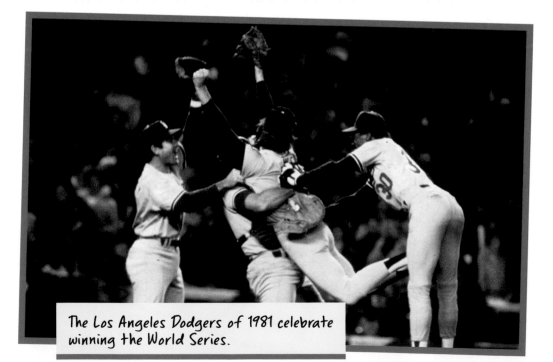

The Los Angeles Dodgers of 1981 celebrate winning the World Series.

But new champions owned the modern era. The most notable was Boston. The Red Sox had not won a World Series since 1918. That was the year before Babe Ruth went to the Yankees. The Sox finally celebrated a title in 2004.

Then they kept rolling. Boston became the most dominant team of the 2000s. They won championships in 2007, 2013, and 2018.

One National League team won 3 World Series in 5 years. They were the Giants. The Giants spent many years in New York.

The New York Giants had last won it all in 1954. They moved to San Francisco in 1958. They lost the World Series in 1962, 1989, and 2002. But once they started winning, they made it a habit. The San Francisco Giants won the World Series in 2010, 2012, and 2014.

Willson Contreras runs the bases in 2016 for his team, the Chicago Cubs. 2016 was the year the curse was broken! The Cubs won the World Series.

The famous Wrigley Field in Chicago is home to the Chicago Cubs.

Many Chicago Cubs fans believed their team was cursed. After all, the Cubs had not won a World Series since 1908.

The so-called curse ended in 2016. That year, the Cubs beat Cleveland in the World Series.

That left Cleveland with the longest title drought in baseball. The team hasn't won a Fall Classic since 1948.

AMAZING MOMENT

Heroes of the Fall Classic

The World Series has often made average players famous. It has also featured the best players playing hero.

One was in Game 6 of the 1947 World Series. A defeat that day would have doomed the Brooklyn Dodgers. They were leading 8–5 in the sixth inning. An inning is the period a team is up to bat. Yankees slugger Joe DiMaggio came to bat. He smashed a pitch to deep center field.

DiMaggio's hit seemed to be a home run. That would have tied the game. But unknown Dodgers outfielder Al Gionfriddo sprinted after it. He leaped and snagged the ball. His incredible catch earned the Dodgers the win. But the Yankees came back to win Game 7 and the World Series.

Jackie Robinson was a famous player on the Brooklyn Dodgers. He was the first African American player ever to play in the American or National League. His first game was in 1947.

Albert Pujols of the St. Louis Cardinals hits a home run and takes off to first base!

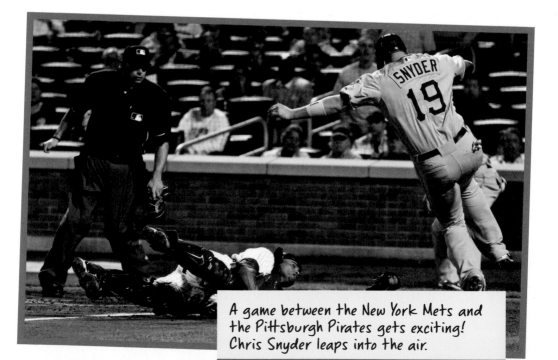

A game between the New York Mets and the Pittsburgh Pirates gets exciting! Chris Snyder leaps into the air.

Don Larsen turned the tables on Brooklyn in 1956. The Yankees pitcher likely would have been forgotten otherwise. He pitched the only perfect game in World Series history. No hitter reached a base against him in Game 5.

Another surprising World Series star was David Freese. He helped St. Louis take the title in 2011. His team was on the verge of defeat against the Texas Rangers. Freese slammed a home run to tie Game 6. Then he blasted another 2 innings later to win it.

Freese was not done leading his team to wins. He really showed his skills in Game 7 with great hits. That helped the Cardinals seal the World Series win.

Through 2021, 117 World Series have been played. And only once did a Game 7 end on a home run.

It was 1960. The Yankees were playing the Pittsburgh Pirates for the championship. The series was tied at 3–3. A crowd of 36,683 packed Forbes Field in Pittsburgh. They watched the teams battle to a 9–9 tie. It was the ninth inning.

Ralph Terry was pitching for New York. Star second baseman Bill Mazeroski stepped to the plate for Pittsburgh. Terry fired a high curveball. This pitch is thrown to make it swerve downward and to the right or left. Mazeroski took a mighty swing. The ball soared over the wall for a home run.

The Pirates had won the Series. Mazeroski was mobbed by fans as he rounded the bases. He was one of the biggest World Series heroes ever. And he did it with just 1 swing of the bat.

Exciting home runs have often spiced up World Series games. One ended what some believe is the best game ever. That was Game 6 in 1975 between the Cincinnati Reds and Boston Red Sox.

Boston needed a win to stay alive. They trailed 6–3 in the eighth inning. But a Bernie Carbo home run tied it.

An even bigger blast was to come. Boston catcher Carlton Fisk sent a towering drive to left field.

Fisk waved his arms to the right. He was trying to will a home run instead of a foul ball. And it was a home run. The Red Sox had won an incredible game. But they lost Game 7 and the title to the Reds.

★ Satchel Paige might have been the greatest pitcher ever. But African American players were not allowed in the MLB until 1947.

★ Paige finally got his chance in 1948. He signed with Cleveland at age 42. And he helped that team reach the World Series.

★ He was amazing. He beat Chicago 1–0 in one game. Nearly 80,000 fans watched it in person. He helped Cleveland get to the World Series. Paige helped his team win the title.

LEGENDS OF THE SPORT

Activity

Go online and read about your favorite baseball team. Learn about charity work a player does to help people. Find out what he does to make the world a better place. Then ask your teacher if you can write about it.

Learn More

BOOKS

Herman, Gail. *What Is the World Series?* New York: Penguin Workshop, 2015.

Jones, Tyler. *The Awesome Baseball Activity Book for Kids*. Independently Published, 2020.

MacKinnon, Adam C. *Baseball for Kids: A Young Fan's Guide to the History of the Game*. Emeryville, CA: Rockridge Press, 2020.

WEBSITES

Horace Mann: World Series Fun Facts: https://www.horacemann.com/teacher-lounge/resources-for-educators/marketing-articles/world-series-fun-facts

MLB Kids: https://www.mlb.com/fans/kids

Sports Illustrated Kids: Baseball: https://www.sikids.com/baseball

Glossary

broadcast rights (BRAWD-kast RYTZ) legal agreement to earn money from a game aired on radio or TV

curveball (KUHRV-bawl) baseball throw intended to swerve downward in one direction

dead ball (DEHD BAWL) a baseball that does not travel very far

dynasty (DYE-nuh-stee) period in which the same team wins many titles

inning (IH-ning) period in a baseball game when one team is at bat

pennant (PEH-nuhnt) league championship

perfect game (PUHR-fikt GAYM) game in which the pitcher does not allow any member of the other team to reach first base

playoffs (PLAY-awfs) series of games that determine World Series teams

Index

About the Author

Marty Gitlin is a sports book author based in Cleveland. He won more than 45 awards as a newspaper sportswriter from 1991 to 2002. Included was a first-place award from the Associated Press for his coverage of the 1995 World Series. He has had more than 200 books published since 2006. Most of them were written for students.